13 Tips to Becoming the Light of Christ

Matthew Robert Payne

Please visit *http://personal-prophecy-today.com* to sow into Matthew's writing ministry, to request a personal prophecy or life coaching, or to contact him.

Editing by Lisa Thompson at *www.writebylisa.com*. You may contact Lisa via email at *writebylisa@gmail.com* for your editing needs.

Book design by Wendy at WildBlu Design. You may contact Wendy via email at *wendy@wildbludesign.com*.

Published by Christian Book Publishing USA. The opinions expressed by the author are not necessarily those of Christian Book Publishing USA. Christian Book Publishing USA is committed to excellence in the publishing industry.

Paperback ISBN: 978-1-925845-06-8

First Edition: October 2018

0 1 2 3 4 5 6 7 8 9 1 0

Dedication

I dedicate this book to my author friend, Michael Van Vlymen. He pursues God with all that is within him and is a great example to all of us. I count it an honor to know Michael, and I am so happy that I can talk to him from time to time over the phone. Everyone should have a person that they look up to as a friend. You can find his books online.

A Note from My Editor

Dear Reader,

Many of you might have begun a relationship with Christ, but you aren't sure where to go from here. You are wondering about practical ways to share your faith and influence those around you. In this little book, you will find thirteen ways that you can become the light of Christ to others. While you might have thought of some of these, others are not quite as obvious. Read each one with thought and prayer as to how you can apply that tip to your life.

You will find another benefit from applying these pointers to your life: you will grow in strength and personal victory in your own relationship with God. You see, these are not just tips so that you can be a light to others. They will point you to Jesus and draw you much closer to him.

Just a little preview from my end—my favorite tip is number six, releasing forgiveness. We often underestimate the power of forgiveness and how much freedom it brings to us.

If you have any editing needs, I would be happy to help. You can learn more about me at my website at *www.writebylisa.com* or by emailing me directly at *writebylisa@gmail.com.*

Happy reading and blessings to all!

Lisa

Table of Contents

Tip 1:
Being the Tree of Life

I will quote Psalm 1:1–3 here, and then we will start. "Blessed is the man who walks not in the counsel of the ungodly, nor stands in the path of sinners, nor sits in the seat of the scornful; but his delight is in the law of the Lord, and in His law he meditates day and night. He shall be like a tree planted by the rivers of water, that brings forth its fruit in its season, whose leaf also shall not wither; and whatever he does shall prosper."

If you want the promise in this scripture, you need to obey what the passage is saying at the very beginning.

"Blessed is the man who does not walk in the counsel of the ungodly." If people are doing things that are ungodly, if people are not Christians, for instance, you don't have to walk in their counsel. You should be taking your counsel and directions from godly people, Christian people. You need to surround yourself in life with people who are friends, who are intimate with you. They don't give you ungodly counsel nor do they stand in the path of a sinner.

You don't want to surround yourself with people who block others from coming into the kingdom of God. Certain Christians engage in such behaviors. They stand in the path of sinners.

You don't want to surround yourself with people who block others from coming into the kingdom of God. Certain Christians engage in such behaviors. They stand in the path of sinners.

Do not walk in the counsel of the ungodly nor stand in the path of sinners nor should your life reflect the kind of life that discourages people from the Christian faith. Nor should you sit in the seat of the scornful. Another translation uses the term mockers.

Mockers are people who have nothing better to do than to mock the pastor, pull down Christians, speak scornfully, mock others, walk in pride, and be full of themselves. I used to hang out with ungodly people who were bearing a bad witness to the Christian life. This means I stood in the way of the sinner, and my friends were mockers. They mocked Christian leadership and other Christians, and they were full of gossip and slander.

God impressed this verse upon me and called me out of those friendships. I went from having friends to having no friends. I just had Jesus as my friend because he called me away from them. "Blessed is the man who doesn't do those things, but his delight is in the law of the Lord and in his law, he meditates day and night." The law of the Lord to David was the written law of the Torah, the commandments of God, but today we can take David's words to include the whole Bible.

One of the ways you can become the light of Christ in this world is to meditate on the Bible day and night. One interesting point is that you don't have to be reading your Bible every day, but you certainly want to be contemplating regularly on scripture and meditating on certain verses.

One way to explain what meditation is like is a cow that chews its cud. The process involves the cow chewing the grass and then swallowing and then regurgitating it in a sloppy mess. Then the cow chews and swallows it again, mixes it with stomach acid and regurgitates it and then chews it again. That's symbolic of meditating on scripture. You need to take scripture and chew on it and get all the meaning you can from it. Let it drop down into your stomach, into your spirit, and then regurgitate it and bring it up to your mind again and think on it and ponder it and question it, and then let it settle back down in your spirit. This process of meditation is what David's talking about. This is meditating on scripture day and night.

I wrote a book called *Nineteen Scriptures to Change your Life Forever* The book is full of all the scriptures that I've meditated on for many years. You can read that book with the scriptures and see what I have learned about them over the years. If you meditate day and night, you should "be like a tree planted by the rivers of water, that brings forth its fruit in season, whose leaf also shall not wither; and whatever he does shall prosper" (Psalm 1:3).

You become like a righteous tree of life. You become a tree planted by the rivers of water, which stands for the Holy Spirit. You are situated next to a river of the Holy Spirit, and your roots are watered by that river. This is a sort of tree that bears its fruit in season whose leaf does not wither. In other words, there's no seasonal drop off of brownness of the leaf. The tree always bears leaves. It's always green, sustained, and always beautiful. It brings forth its fruit in the right season.

You can have answers for people. If someone needs money, you will have it for them. If someone needs help changing a tire, you can change a tire with the person. If someone needs a listening ear, you're there to listen. You have all the fruit of the Spirit, which is bound up in love and compassion for people. You can practically be a tree of life for someone. When they have a problem, they can come to you, and you will have a solution for them.

The last part of the verse says, "Whatever he does shall prosper." Imagine living a life of favor, a life where God blesses every step that you take and every decision that you make. Everything that you do is led, orchestrated, and blessed by God, and you are blessed with favor in whatever you do.

This is what "whatever you do shall prosper" means. Do what this verse says. The first key is not to walk in the counsel of the ungodly, not to stand in the path of sinners, nor to take a seat with the mockers and the scornful. You should meditate on the scriptures day and night and read the scriptures so that they become living and breathing within you. Then you'll become the living tree of life that provides sustenance and blessing to everyone around you. Everyone that you do life with and whatever you put your hand to will prosper. I can say that I'm living that life, according to this verse, which I've meditated on for over twenty years. The verse has come off the page now and is now part of my life.

Tip 2:
Putting Your Trust in God and Not Man

Jeremiah 17:7–8 says, "Blessed is the man who trusts in the Lord, and whose hope is the Lord. For he shall be like a tree planted by the waters, which spreads out its roots by the river, and will not fear when heat comes; but its leaf will be green, and will not be anxious in the year of drought, nor will cease from yielding fruit."

This is the picture of a person who puts his trust in the Lord. This scripture also says that this person is blessed, blessed to trust in the Lord. This is contrary to trusting in man, in popular teachings, in popular doctrines, and in the teachings of men. This person trusts God and puts their hope in the Lord.

You not only trust the Lord with your life, but all your hope is in him. So many people say they have a relationship with the Lord, but they don't currently hear from him, and he doesn't speak to them. They might think that they have a great relationship with the Lord, but they can't tell you anything about him, about his personality, about what he's thinking, or about what he likes and dislikes. They just don't know the Lord.

In order to trust the Lord, you need to come to a place where you obey him. When you do, you'll realize that he is smart and that his ways are smart. When you realize how smart he is, then you have more faith in him, and you trust the Lord. And when you trust him, you'll obey him more.

When your trust and hope are in the Lord, you'll be like a tree planted by the waters, which represents the waters of the Holy Spirit. This is such a great way to live. It's rich by the river, which means that you're being fed by the riverbank.

When heat or drought comes to the land, when depression comes into life, when trials and hardships happen, when dangerous times come, you won't feel them. You won't be troubled, but your leaf will be green all season. The leaves on your tree will be green no matter the time of year. You won't go through a season of autumn when the leaves fall off. Your tree will always be green, and you won't be anxious in the year of drought.

When hard and oppressive times come, you'll be able to stand and be strong and be just as bold and courageous as you are when everything is going well. You'll be just as bold and courageous in hard times. Nor will you cease from yielding fruit. You won't yield fruit and then yield less fruit during a drought. You will always be yielding fruit. You'll always be a blessing to everybody around you. People will come to you in the year of drought for your fruit, and you'll be able to supply them with food.

That is compared to a person who puts their trust in man. This type of person is explained in Jeremiah 17:5. "Cursed is the man who trusts in man and makes flesh his strength." So many people depend on their jobs, on their own decisions, or on men and women in government to make their decisions. They act in the flesh and are not led by the Holy Spirit in the decisions they make. They instead trust their logic, thinking, and reasoning. They don't have a relationship with Jesus or with the Holy Spirit to be led in what decisions to make. They're making fleshly decisions and are led by their flesh. They trust in men.

Many people don't have an intimate relationship with the Lord. They start to trust their job and their earning capacity. They start to trust the people that they know instead of trusting the Lord.

Jeremiah 17:6 says, "For he shall be like a shrub in a desert and shall not see when good comes." Good can come to this person, but they might not even recognize it. This is like the people of America when Donald Trump has come to the country, and half of America can't say that it's positive. They put their trust in men, and so when they put their trust in their own flesh, they can't see when the good comes. When good things happen to this person, they can't see it.

Jeremiah 17:6 continues, "But shall inhabit the parched places in the wilderness, in a salt land which is not inhabited." This person is compared to someone living in a desert in a parched land where there's no water and no healthy environment for good living. They don't have a place to spring up and have a fruitful and an abundant life.

Jeremiah was trying to paint this picture of a person, comparing them to a tree, a person who puts his trust in man. This person has hardships, is planted in the desert, doesn't bear fruit in its season, and doesn't yield fruit all year round. This person is compared to someone who is planted and supported by God whose leaf is always green. This person makes their flesh their strength and relies on men and is always frustrated with problems and troubles. They are always struggling and looking to men, so the favor of the Lord is not in their life even with other people. They are totally controlled by the whims of society and the world and the hardships of this life.

Will you put your trust in God, or will you put your trust in man? You might need to ask yourself this question. That's one of the ways that you can become the light of Christ.

Tip 3:
Being the Light of the World

Matthew 5:14–16 says, "You are the light of the world. A city that is set on a hill cannot be hidden. Nor do they light a lamp and put it under a basket, but on a lampstand, and it gives light to all who are in the house. Let your light so shine before men, that they may see your good works and glorify your Father in heaven."

I was out prophetically evangelizing today. As I was going out, I asked the Lord for an opportunity to give a prophetic word to someone. I was attracted to a certain girl as the Holy Spirit illuminated her, and he told me that he had a prophetic word for her. I approached her and said, "Excuse me, I have a gift. From time to time, that gift allows me to have a message for a person. Today I have a message for you."

She looked appreciative, and then I gave her a prophetic word. I later learned that she was a member of a megachurch in Sydney, Australia, Hillsong. This church produces music around the world, and they have many successful, thriving churches.

This church was founded on this verse that a city on a hill cannot be hidden. They wanted their songs to go around the world as if they were shouted from a hill. You can become so popular in your ministry and in your life that you can make a YouTube video that goes viral so that twenty million people see it. You can demonstrate your life in such a way that it affects more than just your own community.

Jesus says that we are the light of the world. When he was here, Jesus was the light of the world, but then he passed the baton, like in a relay race, to us. He's asked us to take up the baton and become the light of the world. He says that no one lights a lamp and puts it under a basket, but we put it on a lampstand so that it gives light to the whole household. He says, "Let your light so shine that men see your good works and give glory to the Father in heaven."

We should live a life that is so laid down, so humble, and so full of God's love and compassion that people see the light of Christ in us.

People need to see Jesus in us. People are used to the selfishness of this world and are used to people making themselves number one. When they come across a helpful, generous, kind, loving, compassionate person who's giving, humble, peaceful, and joyful, they come across something that they haven't encountered before. They see it especially well when there's a little bit of friction. For example, a positive attitude is obvious when a person is called to do all the dirty work and hard work in their job. They can see the difference in the attitude if the person has been given a challenging job. People recognize when a Christian does their work unto the Lord and then pays attention to other workers. That person blesses other workers and can be depended on to do the hard work, pitch in, and get the job done. The people of the world are looking for those who are different.

When you're laughing, upbeat, happy, kind, good, joking, encouraging, and complimenting others on their work and on how they carry themselves, you make a difference to people. This is the light that people are looking for.

Jesus wants to live in you. He doesn't want to just be someone you worship on Sunday. He wants to take over your life and fill you so that you demonstrate his love and compassion to a hurting and broken world. He wants you to share Jesus in your workplace, in the shops, in the cafes, and wherever you do your shopping.

There's so much selfishness in the world. When others come across a person who is selfless, humble, kind, loving, and compassionate, they see the difference. The person really shines. Like the verse says, people will see your good works and give glory to God in heaven. People who aren't even Christians will glorify God for the life that you live and exemplify.

Jesus taught here in Matthew 5 just after the Beatitudes that we can be that light, that Jesus has passed his Holy Spirit to us. John 14:12 says that we can do greater works than he did. Not many people understand that verse, which means that we can be like Jesus and do greater works than he did.

One of the things that we can do is share his light. We can demonstrate Jesus and be a living and breathing picture of him to the world. Rather than wondering what Jesus would do in that situation, we need to understand what Jesus taught and how he taught us to behave. Then we need to behave that way in every situation. Rather than just worship Jesus, we need to be Jesus everywhere we go. Every person that we interact with should meet a little Jesus and should see a little Christ in us. We should not be anointed just to do works inside the church. We should carry the anointing and the presence of Christ everywhere that we go.

Tip 4:
Overcoming Disappointment:
When You're Not Called to the Platform

Many people look at the well-known speakers like Joyce Meyer, Benny Hinn, Shawn Bolz, and Bill Johnson. They believe, "Well, this is ministry. This is what the Christian life is all about."

Many people consider these famous preachers to be the epitome of the Christian life. They don't realize all the sacrifices these people went through to get to that place. Many people sadly think that unless they're preaching on a big stage with a huge following like T.D. Jakes, Bill Johnson, or others, they're not worthy. They think unless they have an audience and a big following on YouTube and on Facebook and Twitter, they aren't important. They don't think that they are really accepted as a Christian. They don't really think they're living the best life that they could live. It's a real shame and a lie from the enemy.

My friend Nicola came up with this chapter title, and I think it's very pertinent and much needed in this book.

When you're not called as a well-known speaker, what are you called to be? God calls us to be his light, to be the tree of life mentioned in chapter one and chapter two. He calls us to be encouragers, true forgivers, true friends, and authentic. He calls us to minister to people in our workplace and in our world. He calls us to plant seeds in people's lives that will lead to their eventual salvation. He calls us to serve people and to develop intimacy with Jesus. He calls us to be Christ to everyone who we meet.

I just went through a list of some of the chapters coming up in this book. I have so much to talk about and to tell you. There's so much more for you than how you're currently living, so much more for you to grasp. Just get rid of the feeling that you're a failure unless you're a well-known preacher with a YouTube video that's been seen by millions of people. Renounce the lie that you're not worthwhile. Many prophets will never be known internationally or even on a national scale. Many prophets are serving a church and have just prophesied to a few people. They have given a prophetic word at their church but aren't known outside those circles.

Many prophets will minister to the Lord and to people from here and there but won't make a big impact in the world. But they will make a big impact on God and are personal friends with him. They do a lot of prayer and intercede for others.

Many intercessors are hidden in houses and spend hours a day praying for nations and for what God puts on their hearts. Major decisions and breakthroughs in churches, cities, and countries happen because these intercessors are praying. They are praying the burdens that God puts on their heart, and these unseen intercessors make a real difference and are recognized in heaven where they will receive their reward.

They pray in secret. They don't always go to meetings and become intercessors at church. They might be part of the prayer meeting at church, but they might not be recognized as a main intercessor. They are just humble people who make a difference. They make a difference in the world that I live in.

They're not recognized or known this side of eternity. They are just humble, dedicated servants. What do you do? Do you do your job? Do you work at your job and stand out in your workplace? Do people know who you are? Do they know your name? Do they know that you're different? Do you energize and encourage people, making them feel better? How can you make a difference?

I'm now talking to people who are called to the ministry. If you don't end up as a well-known speaker, will you be satisfied just being a prophet in a church, speaking to individuals and encouraging them and, from time to time, releasing a corporate prophetic word in your church? Will you be content if that's what God has for you?

Are you a housewife with a husband and children? Your job is to care for your family and home, which is a big job, by the way, and something I can't do. Do you feel satisfied with your role as a supportive wife and a loving mother to your children? Do you feel loved and appreciated by God? Do you know God in such an intimate way that he can speak to you plainly about what he likes about you and how he can use you?

Are you involved in any way with the church and with the function of your church? Is your role relatively small so that you're not recognized? Are you misunderstood? Do people not get you? Have you been rejected so that you don't feel the love from the Body of Christ? Who are you?

You can be someone different. You can read books and make changes in your life. You can change yourself and bring change into your life in such a way that you can be transformed and have your own personal revival. You can be revived by Christ and become a hot, burning, hungry ember that the Lord can use to intercede or use as a servant to help him build his church in this world.

Do you know your purpose? I wrote a book, *Finding Your Purpose in Christ*, that you can read. You can learn about your purpose. When you find your purpose, you'll be happy to start to walk in it.

Tip 5:
Being an Encourager

Everybody can encourage people. Even if you're an introvert and even if you're not gifted at speaking to people, you can still encourage your friends, people who you're close to and those you know.

One of the best spiritual gifts is the gift of encouragement. I'm not saying that only people with this gift encourage others. A chapter like this would not be worthwhile if I just limited it to people with the gift of encouragement.

How do you encourage people? First of all, you need to have a keen sense of observation. You need to recognize that Julie, the staff member, has never worn that dress before. You need to observe that Peter in your office is wearing a new shirt or a new tie. You should notice that John has on a new suit.

You will recognize these things if you're paying attention. You can tell John, "Dude, that's a nice suit. Is that new?" Or you can pay a compliment to Peter about his shirt or his tie. You can tell Julie that you like her dress.

These are just little things that might seem unimportant to you. But you might find that Julie has had that dress for a year and never felt like she should wear it. One day, she got brave enough to wear it, and now you are complimenting her on how much you like her dress.

Encouragement can be as small as sharing what a great job a person is doing or that you love talking to them because they're such an excellent listener. Encouragement is simply finding a truth about a person and expressing that truth to them in a meaningful way.

I have the gift of encouragement, and I really enjoy encouraging people. Many people tell me that I'm very encouraging. In fact, I prophesied to a couple, a husband and wife, with an international ministry. I send them messages on Facebook, and in his last four messages to me, the husband has said, "Matthew, you are always so encouraging to me."

He is world-renowned in ministry, and he tells me that all my messages to him are so encouraging. People know me as an encourager. When you start to encourage people, you find that it's a real blessing to see something positive in a person and build them up, bringing them happiness and joy. Of course, you might need to develop this skill like any strength. You will need to work at it to improve, which takes practice and perseverance.

I'm sure that many people don't encourage others simply because they feel that they have nothing worthwhile to say. But if you pay attention to people, especially at work, you can just engage them in conversations and thank them for listening to you. Thank them for being so supportive and for their valuable contributions to the conversation.

In church, you can encourage the pastor and tell him or her that you enjoyed the sermon. You can encourage the worship team about the beautiful worship. You can tell the worship leader that you were really encouraged by what she said in between the songs. You can encourage the drummer or the bass guitarist about his gifts and tell him that you really enjoyed the music. If you have an area of expertise, you can encourage people with gifts in that area. You can take the time to learn details about different aspects of ministry and encourage people in those ministries.

You can encourage people by liking and commenting on their posts on Facebook. You can read posts from your friends and make beautiful, encouraging comments. If you don't like how you worded it the first time, you can go back and edit your comment before the person even sees it. You can share their posts or cut and paste them, giving them credit and tagging them so that they can see that you reposted what they said. You can share it on your wall. You feel so uplifted when someone shares your post, and you can be sure it will make another person happy when you share theirs.

You can use Facebook etiquette and like the comments from others on your posts. You can comment on what they say, which really encourages them to engage with your posts. When you put your mind to becoming an encourager, you can find so many ways to encourage people.

Take the time to read through your Facebook page and your newsfeed and read people's posts and like and comment on what they say, encouraging them. Every person wants a certain number of likes (the more the better) on their post. All you have to do is read their post and like it. You can comment at times and engage with the people that you know on Facebook. You'll become a better friend, and you'll be the light of Christ in the lives of the people as you connect on Facebook.

Tip 6:
Releasing Forgiveness –
Your Secret Weapon

I was listening to an apostle teach one time. He never told us he was an apostle. I just figured it out when the Spirit of God told me. He was teaching us that the most important gift that we have is the ability to forgive.

Through the enabling of the Holy Spirit, we have the power to forgive others. People who aren't Christians can't forgive as well as we can. They don't engage with the spirit realm as we do to practice forgiveness as a Christian can.

The apostle said that one of the most powerful tools that we have in our life is the ability to forgive. He said, "Use this weapon and use it well." People will attack Christians just because they are Christians. They feel that if a person is a Christian, they should act a certain way. So they'll purposely treat you badly to see how you'll react.

As a Christian, you have the power to forgive. As a Christian, you have the ability to forgive others and say and act like you forgive them and treat them as if nothing has happened. Not many people will continue to act badly toward you when you continue to forgive them. It's your heart that matters. The way that you feel matters.

Forgiveness can become a powerful weapon, especially when it's combined with love and compassion toward the other person. You can show humility, consideration, and kindness toward the person. If they continue to hurt you or act out toward you, and you keep forgiving them, it can be a powerful force in that person's life.

You might never see these results. You might not see the person quit their rude behavior and stop treating you badly. You might leave that workforce without ever knowing that the person became a Christian, but you can have peace that if they know that you're Christian and if you continue to forgive them and respect them and speak well toward them, you might have an impact on them. That's how you become the light of Christ. Walking in forgiveness is one of the easiest ways to become the light of Christ in a person's life.

This might be a hard lesson for some people. There's a lot of spiritual warfare in the world. Satan certainly uses people, even when they don't know it, to attack and act out against Christians. People who aren't Christians have no understanding that demons use them as puppets to hurt you and cause you struggles. You can be the better person, the person who walks on solid ground by forgiving and loving. You can reward someone's aggression with love, compassion, and humility.

If you can't forgive, you might struggle with pride. That might be hard for some people to hear, but self-pity and striving comes from a root of pride in our lives. Some of the proudest people in the world have the lowest self-esteem. You wouldn't think a person with low self-esteem is prideful, but they find one thing that they are good at and boast to everyone about how good they are. They become very prideful, but they are hurting and struggling with self-esteem issues.

People who are struggling will act out, especially against others who they view as weaker. They believe these people will accept their abuse. In some ways, we can act like victims as Christians, but I'm not encouraging you to act like a victim. I'm recommending that you set healthy boundaries and act responsibly with people. Use that secret weapon of forgiveness and see it work wonders in your life and in the lives of those you interact with and do business with.

Tip 7:
Being a True Friend

Proverbs 18:24 tells us, "A man who has friends must himself be friendly, but there is a friend who sticks closer than a brother."

A true friend is closer than a brother and can be even closer than a real blood brother. I pray that you have friends like this in your life.

How can you be a true friend to a person? Friendship sometimes takes years to develop, and the one commonality with deep friendship is time spent with a person. The more time you spend with a person, the closer your friendship becomes.

Another aspect of a close friendship is honesty and transparency. If you're honest and transparent with your friends, you develop a level of trust and respect with them. These are qualities and key elements that you can apply to being a friend, a true friend.

You don't have to be on the same economic level to be friends. Being the light of Christ is being a friend to all kinds of people from all walks of life. Like me, you can be on a disability pension and have friends who are drug addicts, homosexuals, pastors, preachers, and prophets on the internet.

You can be on a disability pension and write fifty-one books and be friends with some of the people who have read all your books, like Nicola and Mary. I'm friends online with people who have read all my books. A year ago, they contacted me and wanted to know me better. I had the time in my schedule to develop friendships with people.

Let me tell you about my friend Mary. I'll just use her as an illustration of what a true friend is like. She has read forty-nine of my books as of the publishing of this book, which is all but two of my books. She writes a great review on each book she reads. She's my number one reviewer, and she has so much to talk to me about.

She has a lot going on in her life, and she's very enjoyable to talk to. She's a great friend to me. She knows my weaknesses. She knows the addictions and sins that I've struggled with. She knows my transparency when I've fallen into sexual sin. She understands that and prays for me and prays for healing in that area.

We have spent hours and hours talking on the phone together. We've invested time in our relationship. I've been honest and transparent with her. We've established trust between us. I share personal things with her, but she doesn't tell other people. She keeps my confidence.

She is friends with other prophets and apostles, and she brags about me to them. She tells them about me and encourages them to read my books. She's supportive. She's kind. She's generous. She supported a couple of my books and paid for covers to be produced. She's donated to my ministry a few times, but most of all, she listens to me. Most of all, she's there for me. Most of all, she's a friend who really cares about me: my future, my dreams, and my potential.

A friend knows where you've come from, accepts where you are today, and believes in your future. And Mary is a friend like that to me. She accepts my past. She's read my autobiography. She knows the kind of life I've lived. She knows about my future and believes in it. She knows my dreams and aspirations and the prophecies that have been spoken over me. She believes that I can do it, and she accepts me right now as I struggle to overcome sin in my life.

I'm battling in some areas in my life with fitness and eating well. She understands where I'm at now, and she believes in me and prays for me. This is what makes a true friend.

When you want to become the light of Christ, you might want to become that authentic, true friend to someone. You have time for your friend and are honest and transparent with him or her. You are generous with your friends, generous with your time and resources.

You treat them just like Mary treats me. She is one of my favorite people in the world. She has earned that right through many great conversations and many things that she's done. She follows, likes, comments, and shares my posts on Facebook. She does all the things that I talk about that you need to do when encouraging people. She does all of those things for me. She tells me when she likes one of my videos. She tells me what she likes about each individual book that she reads.

She's very giving, and in the same way, I'm giving to her. I listen to her. I encourage her. I bless her. I don't think I bless her as much as she blesses me, but she might argue with me over that point! She feels tremendously blessed to be my friend, and like any friendship, both parties should feel really blessed to be the friend of the other. If one party feels deserving of the other person's friendship, a bit of pride might be involved. One of the tips to becoming the light of Christ is to be a true friend to people.

Tip 8:
Being Authentic:
Demonstrating Integrity, Honesty, and Humility with People and God

God knows us, knows every sin we've committed. Some would argue and say he doesn't know every sin we've committed because he's cast all our sins into the sea of forgetfulness. I'd have to agree with that, but he knows our weaknesses and our struggles. He knows our potential. He knows everything about us. Somehow many of us fail to be authentic with God.

Instead we hide from him—a lot. This affects our relationship with him and how we live our lives when we're not authentic with him. God wants us to be vulnerable and real with him. He wants us to love him, not as slaves but as those who are willing to be obedient to him and follow in his ways. His ways are really the best ways.

When we're sinning, we're harming ourselves. We're not really harming God unless we're hurting another person, but many times, sin *is* hurting another person. I guess I'm wrong there. God wants us to be authentic and real with him, and he wants us to approach him with integrity, honesty, and humility.

Can we do that? Can we be authentic with God? Are you authentic with him? One of the ways to becoming the light of Christ is to reach a stage of intimacy with the Father so that you can be real with him, that you can let your hair down, that you can discuss the nitty-gritty details of your life. He wants you to be able to relax. He doesn't want you to strive or to put on a pretense.

He doesn't like long-winded or eloquent prayers but wants us to pray from the heart. Your own father wouldn't want you to come to him with memorized words. He wouldn't want you to talk formally with him. He would just want you to be real with him. The same is true with God, your Father.

A real father wouldn't like you putting on airs and graces when you come into his presence. A real father wouldn't like you speaking long-winded sentences to him. He just wants you to be real and have honest dialogue with him. The same is true of God. So many people think God is different from a natural father. Well, they are right. God *is* different from a natural father. He is better. Kinder. Wiser. More loving. He's everything a natural father should be but so much more. Many people don't treat God like a natural father. They treat God as if he's not as good as their own father, and that's simply wrong.

God wants us to have integrity with him, to be a person of our word. When we make him a promise, he wants us to carry out the promise, even if it comes at personal cost to us, even if the situation changes, and it's hard for us to keep the promise. He wants us to walk with him with integrity, be honest with him, share our hearts with him, and be transparent with him. If we're struggling to do something for him, he wants us to share and discuss it with him and talk about it so that we can find a solution that works for both of us.

Sometimes you can't talk it through or find a solution. Sometimes the solution is to go through with what you promised him in the beginning. He wants us to walk in humility and admit that we were wrong. He wants us to know that we're human and fraught with failures. We have limitations, and he wants us to be humble and not proud of who we are.

One way to become the light of Christ is to become vulnerable. Recognize that you are a humble servant and deal with God with authenticity, flowing from your relationship with God. He wants you to have authentic relationships and be real, honest, humble, and walk in integrity with others. He doesn't want you to be proud.

One reason that I am open about the sexual sin in my life is to humble myself before you and to walk in integrity. As readers, you can see that I still struggle with some issues. It's all right for me to admit that I still struggle because I do, and I will say what the Holy Spirit leads me to say. He led me to confess my shortcomings here.

I still have struggles. I'm overweight and am on a diet and am exercising to lose weight. I still struggle with that and with walking more than ten minutes. I have struggles in my life. God wants us to be real, honest, and transparent with people. He doesn't want you to think that I'm better than you in any way. He doesn't want you to think that I'm more advanced than you are or that I have fewer problems than you do. He wants you to know that I'm a person just like you are. I have my issues and struggles in life just like you do. He wants you to be honest and humble and walk in integrity with people. He wants you to be a person of your word with others. When you say you're going to do something, he wants you to follow through.

Many people don't keep their word these days. They make promises that they don't keep. They're not honest. They don't treat people with humility or carry themselves with humility. This book takes humility to write, to speak, and then to transcribe into an actual book.

It takes time, effort, and money to create books. I've only been inspired to produce this book because I know it'll be encouraging to you, the reader. Be sure that you're authentic with God and people.

Tip 9:
Ministering to People
at Work and in Your World

As of the writing of this book, I am on a disability pension from the government, so I don't work for a living. I do prophecy requests and messages from angels for people for donations. People also support my book-writing ministry with donations as my books only cost ninety-nine cents. People just want to donate money for me to produce more books. I don't have a job except for ministry, so I don't interact in the workplace with people anymore. I used to work, and I'll share some information in this chapter about the job that I used to have. I just want to be clear with you that I work full-time in ministry for the Lord. My current income comes from a disability pension from the government. I don't legally have to work for the rest of my life.

My pension is similar to an old-age pension, but it's a disability pension. I don't work. That's new information to some people.

But I worked in the past. I used to work as a kitchen hand, washing dishes and assisting chefs in kitchens. I used to work as a temporary employee and go from kitchen to kitchen washing dishes and doing odd jobs. I was a bright light everywhere I went. I was happy. I engaged with the chefs and with the workers in the workplace. I was just a happy soul. Sometimes I developed a closer relationship with the people I worked with as I cut up vegetables and helped and assisted chefs. I engaged people in conversations.

People sometimes found out that I was a Christian through some of our conversations. But sometimes people didn't find out I was a Christian. I was a positive influence. When I went back to certain locations for the second and third time, I built relationships with people. One of my best memories was when I was hired to return to the same kitchen with a German chef, Hans. Hans understood that my hands had a tremor. He used to hire me as a salad hand, which is like an assistant chef. He knew that my hands shook. He picked certain jobs for me to do during the day that my hands could manage, such as taking out sausages, placing them in pans, cooking a barbecue, and doing whatever my hands could manage.

He was a kind boss. He understood my limitations and picked appropriate jobs for me to do in his kitchen. I really influenced others. I brought joy to people and encouraged them. I told people great stories. I had a few people question me about my Christian faith. I witnessed to a witch, someone who was starting to dabble in witchcraft. She asked me if I could be her boyfriend, and I had a strong testimony with her. I told her, "If we become boyfriend and girlfriend, we can't have sex."

She answered, "What's the point of being in a relationship if you can't have sex?" She was surprised at how I witnessed to her. I was really surprised that I didn't succumb to this pressure in my walk at that time.

In your workplace, you can be an encouragement and a shining light to people. You can demonstrate Jesus to them. You can be positive, loving, kind, and generous.

You can work hard at your job, work extra hours, and work overtime when needed. You can work off the clock for certain reasons. You can make a practice of working half an hour and not be paid when you need to help out.

When you go the extra mile at your workplace, put in the extra effort, and do an exemplary job of everything that you say and do, you are a positive influence. Be the person who stands out as one who doesn't complain or gossip or spread rumors. Be the person who encourages and blesses people with everything that you say and do.

As you engage with others in your world—at the gas station, the grocery store, the café, restaurants, and more—ask your cashier or server about their day. Ask what they like to do when they're not at work. When you see them again, ask how they enjoyed their recreation. Ask about their favorite TV shows. Engage with them if you watch those shows.

Let people who serve you know that they're important to you. It's not just the coffee they're serving you or the food that they're selling you that matters. Their life is important to you, and you care about them and love them. Engage with people that you do life with, that you interact with, and encourage them and ask questions. People like to answer questions about themselves. You can ask all sorts of people questions about themselves, and they love to answer.

One way to easily carry on a conversation is just to ask plenty of questions. When they answer you, ask them a question about their answer and dig deep with people. You'll find that people will really love you, and you'll shine the light of Christ everywhere you go as you interact with others.

Tip 10:
Planting Seeds in People's Lives

You can plant seeds in people's lives by letting them know that you're a Christian. You can easily do this by saying, "Yesterday when I was at church, someone said this," or "My pastor said this at church last week," or "Tomorrow at church, I'm going to a sing this song and lead worship." You can mention something about church, about what you've read in the Bible, or about your Christian faith.

You don't have to say, "Hi, I'm a Christian. I want to convert you." You can just bring your Christian life into the current conversations that you have. Someone might say something, and you'd mention your pastor or talk about church. It's just a casual comment, but it lets them know that you're a Christian.

As you shine the light of Christ, you are planting seeds in that person's life. They're seeing an authentic Christian, someone real before them, displaying the Christian faith. You're an example of a Christian to them.

Another way to plant seeds in people's lives is through acts of generosity and kindness. People sometimes have to move to another house. Rather than pretending that you didn't hear that they have to move, you can ask them if they need help. You can volunteer to cook for someone when someone's spouse goes into the hospital. You can look for ways to serve people with random acts of kindness. You can always look for ways to help and encourage people and be a blessing to them. Those ways can be as creative as you are.

You can ask people if they go to the movies, and next time you're at the movies, maybe you can buy them a gift card. You can just bless them. When they ask why, you can tell them, "Just for being a nice person. Thanks for being my friend. I appreciate you, and I want to show you that with these movie tickets."

You can plant seeds in people's lives in so many ways. One way that I do this is through the gift of prophetic evangelism. I walk up to people and say, "Excuse me, I have a gift at times that allows me to receive a message for a person. Today I have a message for you."

Then I'll just launch into a prophetic word, which totally stumps people and blows them away. Well, I've planted the seed. By the end of it, I'll tell them that God told me what to say, and the message is from Jesus, and he loves them. I've planted the seed in their life, and Jesus can later bring another Christian to them to water it. They can remember that prophetic word that I gave, especially when it comes true.

I've written a book called *Prophetic Evangelism Made Simple: Prophetic Seed Sowing*. You can look up that book and teach yourself how to prophesy and learn how to do prophetic evangelism. That's one way to plant seeds in people's lives.

Through the gift of encouragement and through being authentic, you can learn how to interact with people at work. You can interact with those you do life with, such as cashiers or servers, and you can let them know in conversation that you're a Christian. Then you can just love on them. Shower them with love, with compliments, with blessings, with encouragement, and just be a friend to these people.

Soon enough, you will have planted some seeds that God can work on. Soon enough, you'll have people asking you questions, asking you to pray for them, or inquiring about your Christian faith.

One way to engage further with people is to ask them if they have any needs that you can pray for when you're praying at home. Often people will receive prayer, and they will give you a prayer request. You can watch God answer that prayer request and see a new convert to the Christian faith.

Being the light of Christ comes very simply and naturally to me. I hope that as you read this book and as you go through these pages, you come to realize that you, too, can be the light of Christ. You, too, can have an impact and plant seeds in people's lives.

Tip 11:
Serving People through Acts of Service

We mentioned briefly before that if someone was moving, you could offer to help them move. This need might come up every year or so if you have a lot of friends. People sometimes get sick and go to the hospital, and you can cook a meal for the family. If you're a male, you can have your wife cook a meal if you can't cook. Or you might buy them a gift card to a local restaurant.

You can serve people in many ways: help with their workload in the office, train others at work, help with shopping, carry groceries, and more. You can look for opportunities to serve others everywhere you go.

So many functions in a church need attention with many jobs that need to be done. I'm sure that not many people sign up to clean the toilets. You could offer your services as the cleaner. You could help prepare communion or arrange the flowers at church. You can go to the minister and ask him how you can help and tell him why you think you can help. You could help the minister with anything that he asks you to do.

Ministers don't always need your finances. You can learn to serve ministers in so many ways. Some friends are removing junk outside my house that's been there for years, stuff I've slowly collected that I no longer want. According to housing regulations, these items need to be removed within fourteen days. A couple of church friends will come by with a van to haul all that stuff away. I'm so grateful and so happy for this act of service. I can't repay this debt, and it just shows how much they love me.

Months ago, when I joined the church, they totally changed my house. They bought me a new bed and a new sofa. They changed my lightbulbs, bought new cupboards, and hung the pictures on my walls. They did a whole lot of odd jobs at my house out of love. They didn't charge me anything. They didn't want any money. They just wanted to love me.

These men provide housing for students from Nepal. They find the housing for students and search for furniture for the houses. They move it to the houses. They do this as an act of service.

Their names are Tofan and David, and I'll mention them in this book because I'm really blessed by what they have done for me. I can't repay them. All I can do is love them more deeply than I love them. That's how you can affect people. You can do acts of service for people. You can help them in any way possible. They will feel indebted to you and feel like they're really being loved.

This is the way to plant seeds in people's lives and help people soften to the gospel of Jesus Christ. By doing acts of service and acts of love for others, you really become the light of Christ for a person. You shine brightly with the light of Christ, and people can't deny it. When they are left in your debt, there's nothing they can do. They almost want to become a Christian just because of the love that you've shown them.

Tip 12:
Developing Intimacy with Jesus

I wrote a book, *7 Keys to Intimacy with Jesus*, and I'm just going to briefly share these seven keys with you. I hope that you can buy my book. It's only ninety-nine cents, and you can find it in a search.

Key one is obedience. John 14:21 says, "He who has My commandments and keeps them, it is he who loves Me. And he who loves Me will be loved by My Father, and I will love him and manifest Myself to him."

Jesus said in John 14:21 that he who loves me will obey my commands. Jesus says that we love him when we obey his commands. It's important to obey Jesus and what he taught. That's one of the keys to intimacy with Jesus. He and his Father will love the person who obeys his commands. One of the keys to growing in intimacy with Jesus is the walk of obedience.

Of course, when you start to talk to Jesus and learn to hear from him, he starts to tell you to do things. The Holy Spirit starts to direct you in what to do, and you need to do what the Holy Spirit tells you. Obedience is the key.

Key two is prayer. Another key to intimacy with Jesus is prayer. You might be wondering how you can be the light of Christ. I mentioned prayer as important to intimacy with Jesus. You can't grow intimate with Jesus without prayer. Prayer is essential to building an intimate relationship with him.

In chapter one, we talked about meditating on and practicing the Word of God. In this chapter, we're talking about prayer and how important it is to have a strong prayer life.

Key three is asking questions. When you pray to the Lord, you need to learn to have two-way prayer. You need to learn how to pray a prayer and hear from God. I wrote a book, *How to Hear God's Voice: Keys to Conversational Two-Way Prayer*.

As you learn to hear from God, one of the keys to growing in intimacy with Jesus is asking him questions about life, about the Bible, about all kinds of things. You connect with God and Jesus in the same way that you connect with a friend: meeting for coffee, spending hours and hours in conversation, asking plenty of questions, and talking back and forth. Part of the way that you learn to deeply know a person is to ask them questions.

One of the keys to intimacy with Jesus isn't just a one-way prayer to Jesus or to God but a two-way prayer that includes asking Jesus questions. You can be really touched.

Key four to intimacy with Jesus is having the right theology. You can be a Christian and be very religious, believing that the Old Testament is still true today and that all the laws of the Old Testament must be obeyed. You can be really strict and focused on judgment and think that God's angry. You can miss the truth of the new covenant relationship and of the love and the grace of God. Missing that truth will stop or impede your growth toward intimacy with Jesus. In order to have true intimacy with Jesus, you need to have your theology in the right place.

As you develop the right theology, which is an understanding of the new covenant and grace doctrine, you will grow into a place where you're intimate with Jesus, and you become the light of Christ in this world.

13 STEPS TO BECOMING THE LIGHT OF CHRIST

Key five is being set apart. Jesus says, anyone that wants to be his friend must first deny his mother, father, sister, brothers, land and possessions in order to possess him. (See Luke 14:26.) Jesus is saying that we need to be set apart.

First John 2:15–17 (NLT) says, "Do not love this world nor the things it offers you, for when you love the world, you do not have the love of the Father in you. For the world offers only a craving for physical pleasure, a craving for everything we see, and pride in our achievements and possessions. These are not from the Father, but are from this world. And this world is fading away, along with everything that people crave. But anyone who does what pleases God will live forever."

This passage says that we're not to love the world or the things of the world or what the world thinks of us, but we're to love God and do what he commands us to do.

This passage commands us to be set apart and to come out of the world, the world's lust, and the world's ways. Enjoy God for who he is and obey God and do what pleases him. You can't grow in increasing intimacy with Jesus if you're still in love with the world.

James 4:4 tells us, "Adulterers and adulteresses! Do you not know that friendship with the world is enmity with God? Whoever therefore wants to be a friend of the world makes himself an enemy of God."

James says here that if you're a friend of the world, you become an enemy of God. In order for you to grow, to be an intimate friend of Jesus, you need to put the world—its ways, its means, and its lust—behind you at some point. You need to go toward Jesus.

Key six is the Word of God. You need to have the Word of God firmly planted in your spirit as we mentioned in tip number one about the tree of life. You need to read and meditate on the Word of God. Once again, I will repeat that the Word of God and an understanding of the scriptures are imperative for you to grow close to Jesus. Jesus is found in the Word of God. The more that you

45

know the Word of God, the more that you understand the Word of God, the closer you become to Jesus Christ.

Key seven is friendships. Like we mentioned in tip number one, you need to leave behind the friendships that are ungodly and the people that are standing in the path of sinners, mockers, and the scornful. You need to leave those bad relationships behind and choose friends that are godly who will encourage you in righteous ways of living and of practicing your faith.

Drawing close to Jesus and developing intimacy with him takes quite a bit of effort. When you put in the effort, you'll become the light of Christ, and it'll be worthwhile. I encourage you to buy *7 Keys to Intimacy with Jesus* and learn more about intimacy.

Tip 13:
Being Christ to People

First John 2:6 says, "He who says he abides in Him ought himself also to walk just as He walked."

The Apostle John is speaking and saying that he who says he abides in Jesus must behave like Jesus. He is saying that he who says that he has a strong relationship with Jesus must walk just as Jesus walked.

Many people don't know that scripture in the Bible. I've never heard a minister preach on it, maybe because it gives us no excuse and commands us to walk like Jesus did in the world. Paul preached and shared the following:

First Corinthians 11:1 states, "Imitate me, just as I also imitate Christ." First Corinthians 4:16 says, "Therefore I urge you, imitate me."

The Apostle Paul said that it was possible to imitate Christ because he was doing exactly that. He was commanding his followers to imitate him just as he imitates Christ. John was saying that whoever says he has a strong relationship with Jesus must walk just as Jesus walked. This is a rather sobering command for all of us and leaves us with no excuses.

You can't justify yourself and say that you're just a human with frailties and that you're just a sinner. You can't make excuses and say that you can't measure up. As a Christian, you have the indwelling power and presence of the Holy Spirit. You have the ability to take every thought captive and decide to do what lines up with the Bible. (See 2 Corinthians 10:4–6.) You have the empowering grace of the Holy Spirit to help you make those decisions. You really can walk and be like Jesus.

My friend Nicola told me that before she met me, she knew that you could read your Bible, but she never realized that you could walk and be like Jesus. She believed that you could do what Jesus did, but she didn't believe that you could behave like Jesus and be Jesus to people. She didn't realize this until she came across my ministry. You can be Christ and demonstrate him to the world and be a living Christ to others.

Jesus wants us to be Christ to people. He wants us to be himself. He wants to possess us. Just like a Jezebel spirit might possess a person and make that person act in a controlling, judgmental, and terrible way to other people, Jesus wants to possess and indwell us through his Holy Spirit so that we fully manifest his personality to the world. He wants us to become the light of Christ and demonstrate Jesus Christ to the world. He wants to demonstrate himself through us to the world.

This is possible. John says that it's possible. It's possible because Paul says so. It's possible because we can do all things through Christ who strengthens us as Philippians 4:13 says. I just want to encourage you that you can really be Jesus Christ to this world. You can really be the light of Jesus to this world.

I hope that this simple book, even though it's short, has been an encouragement to you and blessed you. I hope that it leaves you with an impact that will change and transform your life.

God really cares about you. I really care about you. I want you to listen to this message. I want you to read this message time and time again. I want you to put into practice some of the things

I've said and become the little Christ. Christian means little Christ. I want you to become the little Christ to the world that the world is waiting for. The world is crying out for the love of Christ. The world is crying out for the sons of God to be manifested as Romans 8:19 indicates.

I pray that this book is a blessing to you. I pray that as you read it, you'll understand that you, too, can be the light of Christ, and you, too, can make a difference in this world. You can make a difference by taking the first step.

You can take some of the following steps: ordering the books that I've mentioned in this book and learning how to plant prophetic seeds in people's lives. You can order *Prophetic Evangelism Made Simple: Prophetic Seed Sowing*. You can learn how to hear from God from this book: *How to Hear God's Voice: Keys to Conversational Two-Way Prayer*. You can learn how to have an intimate relationship with Jesus Christ by ordering *7 Keys to Intimacy with Jesus*. You can find your purpose in Christ if you read *Finding Your Purpose in Christ*.

I encourage you to read the resources, put into practice what I say to do, and make the effort to change and become the person you know you are destined to be. You don't have to be a world leader. You don't have to be a popular preacher on a stage. You can just be a small-time Christian. You can just be an average Joe Blow Christian in the world, but you can demonstrate Christ and have his love and compassion for the world, changing the world and impacting it for the greater good.

I'd Love to Hear from You!

One of the ways that you can bless me as a writer is by writing an honest and candid review of my book on the platform from which you purchased it. I always read the reviews of my books, and I would love to hear what you have to say about this one.

Before I buy a book, I read the reviews first. You can make an informed decision about a book when you have read enough honest reviews from readers. One way to help me sell this book and to give me positive feedback is by writing a review for me. It doesn't cost you a thing but helps me and the future readers of this book enormously.

To read my blog, request a life-coaching session, request your own personal prophecy, or receive a personal message from your angel, you can also visit my website at *http://personal-prophecy-today.com* All of the funds raised through my ministry website will go toward the books that I write and self-publish.

To write to me about this book or to share any other thoughts, please feel free to contact me at my personal email address at *survivors.sanctuary@gmail.com*.

You can also friend request me on *Facebook at Matthew Robert Payne*. Please send me a message if we have no friends in common as a lot of scammers now send me friend requests.

You can also do me a huge favor and share this book on Facebook as a recommended book to read. This will help me and other readers.

How to Sponsor a Book Project

If you have been blessed by this book, you might consider sponsoring a book for me. It normally costs me between fifteen hundred and two thousand dollars or more to produce each book that I write, depending on the length of the book.

If you seek the Holy Spirit about financing a book for me, I know that the Lord would be eternally grateful to you. Consider how much this book has blessed you and then think of hundreds or even thousands of people who would be blessed by a book of mine. As you are probably aware, the vast majority of my e-books are ninety-nine cents, which proves to you that book writing is indeed a ministry for me and not a money-making venture. I would be very happy if you supported me in this.

If you have any questions for me or if you want to know what projects I am currently working on that your money might finance, you can write to me at *survivors.sanctuary@gmail.com* and ask me for more information. I would be pleased to give you additional details about my projects.

You can sow any amount to my ministry by simply sending me money via the PayPal link at this address: *http://personal-prophecy-today.com/support-my-ministry.*

You can be sure that your support, no matter the amount, will be used for the publishing of helpful Christian books for people to read.

Other Books by Matthew Robert Payne

What I Believe

Living for Eternity

Your Identity in Christ

7 Keys to Intimacy with Jesus

Finding Intimacy with Jesus Made Simple

Finding Your Purpose in Christ

Jesus Speaking Today

His Redeeming Love: A Memoir (Part 2)

The Parables of Jesus Made Simple: Updated and Expanded Edition

Christian Discipleship Made Simple

Nineteen Scriptures to Change Your Life Forever

Influencing your World for Christ: Practical Everyday Evangelism

Optimistic Visions of Revelation

How to Hear God's Voice: Keys to Conversational Two-Way Prayer

Conversations with God: Book 1

Conversations with God: Book 2

Conversations with God: Book 3

Getting Right with God: Exploring Intimacy through Daily Journaling and the Courts of Heaven

Twenty-Two Signs that You're Called to Be a Prophet

Deep Calls unto Deep: Answering Questions on the Prophetic

A Beginner's Guide to the Prophetic

The Prophetic Supernatural Experience

Prophetic Evangelism Made Simple

My Radical Encounters with Angels

My Radical Encounters with Angels: Book Two

A Message from My Angel: Book 1

Walking under an Open Heaven

My Visits to Heaven: Lessons Learned

Other Books by Matthew Robert Payne *(continued)*

Interviews with the Two Witnesses: Enoch and Elijah Speak

Apostle John Speaks from Heaven: A Divine Revelation

Apostle Paul Speaks from Heaven: A Divine Revelation

Apostle Peter Speaks from Heaven: A Divine Revelation

King David Speaks from Heaven: A Divine Revelation

Mary Magdalene Speaks from Heaven: A Divine Revelation

Mary Magdalene Speaks from Heaven Book 2: A Divine Revelation

Great Cloud of Witnesses Speak

Great Cloud of Witnesses Speak: Old and New

Great Cloud of Witnesses Speak: God's Generals

Great Cloud of Witnesses Speak: Interviews with Martha, Lazarus. Thomas and Timothy

My Visits to the Galactic Council of Heaven

Princess Diana Speaks from Heaven: A Divine Revelation

Michael Jackson Speaks from Heaven

Coping with your Pain and Suffering

Gaining Freedom from Sex Addictions: Breaking Free of Pornography and Prostitutes

Writing and Self-Publishing Christian Nonfiction

Five Keys to Successful Writing: How I Write One Book per Month

Visit Matthew Robert Payne's author page on Amazon at:

https://www.amazon.com/Matthew-Robert-Payne/e/B008N9R896

Upcoming Books

13 Tips to Becoming the Light of Christ

Simple Answers to Your Questions on the Prophetic

Acknowledgments

Jesus:

I want to thank you for being my lifelong friend and for never deserting me, no matter how dark my life became. You led me into some great adventures, such as interviewing saints from heaven.

Holy Spirit:

I want to thank you for leading and teaching me. You are a great teacher, better than I could ever be. You have been with me every step of the way. Even as I do this book, you are with me to still my nerves.

Father:

Thank you for loving me and entrusting me with this life that I am living. Thank you for revealing my purpose to me and leading me toward accomplishing it. Thank you so much for your Son, Jesus. Thank you for everything that you have done in my life.

Lisa Thompson:

I want to give special thanks to Lisa for editing this book of mine. You take my simple words and transform them to make me seem smarter than I really am. If you have any editing needs, Lisa can be contacted at *writebylisa@gmail.com.*

Nicola:

I want to thank my co-author, Nicola, for having the courage to do this book with me. I want to thank you for being part of my team as a proofreader. I want to thank you for all the work that you did with this book to polish and improve it.

Acknowledgments *(continued)*

Friends:

I want to thank Darla, Lisa, Nicola, Mary, Wendy, Laura, David Joseph, and Michael Van Vlymen for your friendship and for how you have impacted my life.

Mom and Dad:

I want to thank my mother and father for all the love that they have given me. I am a product of your love.

Readers and Ministry Supporters:

I want to thank the readers of my books and my ministry supporters for the funds that you have given me to publish books. I want to thank the anonymous ministry supporter who gave me money for this project. I live to educate people, and I thank my readers and the supporters of my ministry because you make life worth living.

About Matthew Robert Payne

A teacher and prophet, Matthew Robert Payne enjoys writing what the Lord puts on his heart. He receives great pleasure from interacting with others on Facebook, hearing from people who have read his books, and prophesying over others. He is a passionate lover and disciple of Jesus Christ. He hopes that as you discover his books, you will intimately come to know Jesus, the Father, and Matthew himself though his transparent writing style.

Matthew grew up in a traditional Baptist church and gave his heart to Jesus Christ at the tender age of eight years old. But when he left home at the age of eighteen, he lived a wild life for many years. At twenty-seven, he was baptized in water and at the same time, baptized in the Holy Spirit. Matthew learned about the five-fold ministry offices and received a revelation of their value today.

He started his journey as a prophet twenty years ago, learning about this gift and putting it into practice. With thousands of prophecies under his belt, he can confidently prophesy to friends and strangers alike. He has been writing for a number of years and self-published his first book in 2011. Today he spends his time earning money to self-publish and writes a new book approximately every month.

Matthew writes simply from his life experience. He picks up information to share in his books from the reading that he does for his own personal growth. He relies on the Holy Spirit to give him verses to share as he writes instead of searching for scriptures to support his points. He is very real, authentic, and honest in his writing and in what he shares with readers.

About Matthew Robert Payne *(continued)*

You can connect with him on Facebook. You can sow into his book-writing ministry, read his blog, receive a message from your angel or even receive your own nine-minute personal prophecy from Matthew at *http://personal-prophecy-today.com.*

www.ingramcontent.com/pod-product-compliance
Lightning Source LLC
Chambersburg PA
CBHW021941040426
42448CB00008B/1183